Dylan Thomas and the Writing Shed

MARTIN WILLITS JR.

FUTURECYCLE PRESS

www.futurecycle.org

Library of Congress Control Number: 2016961613

Published by FutureCycle Press
Lexington, Kentucky, USA

ISBN 978-1-938853-98-2

To my wife, Linda Griggs,
and the people of Swansea, Wales

Contents

I

III

Swansea, Wales

I

The Winner of the Dylan Thomas International Poetry Award

When I won the Dylan Thomas International Poetry Award in 2014, I was invited to go to Dylan Thomas's birthplace in Swansea, Wales, to read my single poem, "Daffodils." The contest was conducted by the University of Wales Trinity Saint David, and the reading was held at the National Waterfront Museum. The program was part of a long celebration of the 100th centennial of Dylan Thomas's birth. "Daffodils" will be on permanent display at the Dylan Thomas Museum.

My poem was chosen from over 350 international poets. The selection committee included Dr. Grahame Davies, Dr. Jeni Williams, and Dr. Menna Elfyn—all three established and published Welsh poets. They compared my poem to the work of William Wordsworth and William Butler Yeats.

Daffodils

Daffodil (*Narcissus pseudonarcissus*)

A daffodil bud is seen among the snow,
offering forgiveness. Winter was harsh,
and the brutality of summer is not far away.
We need forgiveness. Surely, after tribulations
there is relief. Already we are gardening dreams.
It had been huddling like an old gray woman
grabbing her shawl, in an underground house,
stirring a promise to return.
Soon its six petals' harmonic sense will bring love.

All day, it radiates. Although it has not grown,
you can feel the end of winter, like curtains rustling.
It appeared in the Garden of Gethsemane as relief,
and felt what would happen next. It was also there
for the Roman soldiers who bit its bulb to ease
their wounds, knowing what would happen next.

Now it's here for us, and we do not know what will happen.
We only see so far, and things go past faster. Tolerance
is easier as we become older, and suffering becomes normal
as our bodies find new ailments. In our dreams we plant.
We are yellow petals caught in a frayed shawl.

In a world uncertain of what will happen next,
there are some things we can expect and some we can't.
The snow understands it cannot stand in the daffodil's way.

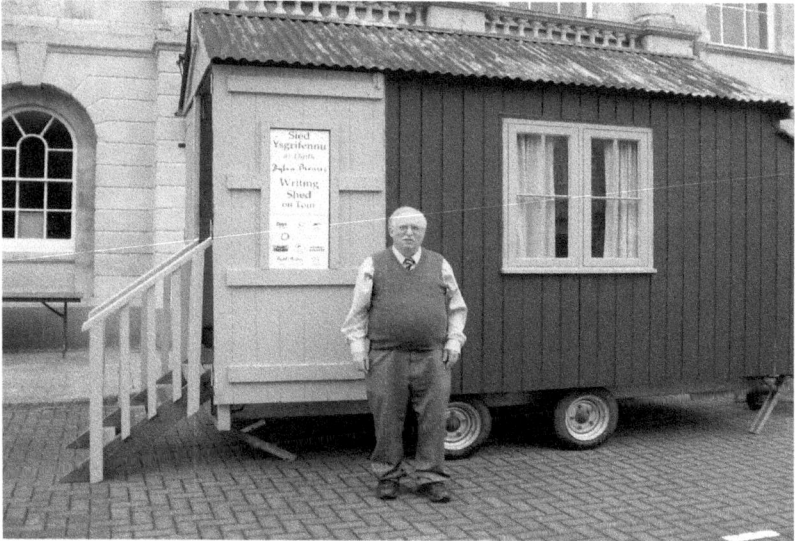

Martin Willitts Jr, before a replica of the Writing Shed

II

Dylan Thomas's Writing Shed and Other Poems

I was able to visit the Dylan Thomas Museum, which had a replica of Dylan Thomas's Writing Shed, in which he wrote many poems towards the end of his life. I visited the Dylan Thomas birth home and saw the park where he played as a child. Along the way, I met Jeff Towns, another Dylan Thomas expert. He sold to me a rare copy of a manuscript he had published of one of Dylan's long-unknown poems with the original Dylan facsimiles across from Dylan's handwriting and corrections.

Dylan Thomas at the Writing Shed

Above the boathouse hill was a shed.
Dylan would find poems like schooners in the bay.
In such a window, no matter how small,
could always see what he needed to see.

From here, he could see the Tâf estuary.
The Gower Peninsula was further beyond
in the Bristol Channel,
the shallows narrowing in.

There were caves in the peninsula
where archeologists found
the Red Lady of Paviland,
a skeleton dyed with red ochre.

He could almost see the menhirs
on the Gower. Those standing stones
had been upright since the Bronze Age,
and now only eight remained.

One was a twenty-five ton capstone
supported with upright stones
like lines stacked to support a poem's meaning.
Anyone could interpret the constructor's intention.

Sometimes all you need are the right tools.
All you needed was all the pain in the world.
After staring, Dylan labored over his poems,
rubbing red ochre into their fragile bones.

Above the Spring Tâf

Painting by Guy Manning

The steep hill towards the sun through the white pine
is where woodpeckers knock searching for insects.
In this spring where you can still feel young,

there is a different kind of silence when sounds
are more intense, where you can hear grass in wind,
singing about the oncoming light rain,
where light itself rains between the drops
tapping on pine needles like tuning forks.

All the absence in your life is filled. There is no need to rush
through damp grass towards sunlight. It will be there
when you need it. Just listen to the katydid
and spring water after ice melt clears its throat.
Above the spring leaves, the stars are greening.
If we climb these hills we might reach them before we die.

Secrets

The yellow flowers make small statements of spring.
They keep their name to themselves,
but proclaim loudly to any who might listen
to look!

Their secrets can only last so long
and then they are gone.

*

If I were to find myself in a field of black-eyed Susans
counting their dark centers
like gateways to recovery from the silence of winter,
then their yellow would enter my blood
like a thousand prayers of peace
awakening that one hidden bell
nobody risked ringing
fearing a possible repercussion
and when it clicks like a cricket
everyone sighs a longing
for what they never knew.

Sometimes, it takes risk to allow changes to happen.

The Boat House and the Dylan Thomas Writing Shed

He would write in a shed near the Swansea Bay.
Salt spray would come through a window,
settle as ink on paper. Gull-cry would go all day,
all night, tidal waves of non-music, more like laughter.

His wife would sunbathe in the back, listening to him write
like a sailboat with no harbor and no fair winds,
all block and tackle, all empty nets full of sadness.
Slickers with rivulets of rain, fog-voice reciting poems
into a stupor deep enough to know seaweeds.

The pots would be empty. The cupboards would be rotten
with silence and cobwebs. All were starving for attention.
The winds would drive fishhooks into him.
He might not notice while waiting for inspiration,
as a sailor waits for a mermaid to seduce him.
Days would be breakers smacking rocks, the stars
would be barnacles on a skiff below waterline,
and his children would know enough not to interrupt him.

In all the years he wandered through Swansea like a banshee
haunting every streetlight, every hill covered by ferns,
did any common person read or know his poems?
Anger rose in him as a swoon of quick storms. It beached
every small boat, it knocked about every sail.
He had imagined every school child, glassblower,
shopkeeper placing an "Open" sign in a window,
widower, and sheep tender in clover fields
knowing his poems by heart. And they did not.

Only the academics wearing scholarly frowns
cared, and he did not care about them. How little
they knew—how sad the nature of man, how
intemperate the winds bringing shiploads of
worthlessness to his door, wanting to enter his skin.

He felt at home in Laugharne or Wind Street
in the No Sign Wine Bar; not with scholars.
O happy is the poet who finds his voice;
how unhappy he is when no one wants to hear it.
He could hear the voices speaking to each other,
great communities of tongues shouting
over each other, rain falling onto rain
as in nasty gale weather when all the seas
forget shores, and the shores forget dry land.

The wind was boastful in the thrashing,
speaking in the old way, the way of graves
and gravel, while he stared into the eye of a storm,
daring it to take him because he had zero
left to give; the rest was taken away long ago,
and he was way past the port of caring.

The Boat House, the graveyard, the writing shack,
all experienced the hunger of isolation. The rush-pulse
sea, the sinking feeling, the waiting for solitude
to stamp its feet before entering and pulling off
wading boots; all were terrible nights growling
with an unfed stomach. The night sea breath of porridge,
planting a kiss on a cheek as an anchor of love,
the smell of gutted fish like a ferry connecting
an island to the mainland through choppy water:
these were familiar to Dylan as words—all mouthfuls
of vowels, all sound and fury and restlessness,
all thrown darts for pints of dark beer.

His words surged back to him as if from a radio.
He recited poems, rattling paper like
turned sails against the wind. He would lower
the shed lights into small fish eyes, plunge the world
into personal darkness. He would speak in a rumble
and clang as a buoy in rough patches.
It all seemed like sunny days never came.

The Writing Shed at the Boat House

To reach this shed, small enough to pace
in a circle tracing Dante's Circle, he had to wind
around the hill, upwards, like a spiral staircase,
staring at the well-worn ground, knowing the ruin
of shoes, the sure-footed user, the way of wind.

If he kept cycling towards heaven,
would he have been happy? What would he find?
The end of his wit? Would he have used the oil lamp?
That one had two switches: the illumination brought insight,
and the off switch, the one of darkness,
troubled everything with reality
of death, the lamp oil taken from a whale.

Was this shed a getaway from himself, or was it
to escape who he had become,
although he had whittled his own image out of straw?

Dylan Thomas in the Writing Shed in Candle Light

Here in the shed he would write
with light from white fingers
of tapered wax-sloughed votive candles
from a Catholic prayer altar,
while the constellation Altar was fire in the sky.

There were pictures cut from newspapers,
with Greta Garbo in direct center,
who, he argued, had no peer.
There was a picture of collapsed castle ruins
like failed poems, torn after two hundred revisions,
scattering as pigeons in a park.

Here he could look out a window, pull the curtains
as intermission for a play, and see what he was missing.
He would wish to join outside, but he had poems to write
and cigarettes to remove from a used cigar box.
He smoked, dragging every last breath of it.
He might open one of the candy wrappers of sourness
to have the taste of reality on his tongue.

He could look out the window
beyond the shadow of blurring lost to sight.

Entering the Dylan Thomas Writing Shed

Today, I step into his shed,
feel the walls like the inside of a whale,
see the images he left behind
like an archeologist's dream.
I see his tweed suit jacket,
and his chair is wearing it
like a king might wear a royal robe,
although his jacket moves as a dream
someone else ought to have.

His shed is writing inside me
with tidal waves of words
crunching as small shells under my feet.

I feel him entering me, his hair wavy as terns
in the skull-opened skies. He is climbing
my backbone like Jacob's Ladder
or a staircase of a lighthouse
to shine into the worst kind of fog.

Here is a list of vocabulary words,
searching for the precise meaning,
the perfect word, the kind of word
that disappears into a lawyer's contract
everyone signs but no one ever understands.

Here is the moon, the burning end of a cigarette.
Here is the haphazard sketching of seas
changing the handwriting on the sand.
Here I see myself in the reflection of large eyes
staring back, asking where I have been
all these years. I speak as if into a microphone
during a report about a blitzkrieg.
I put on the tweed because it is suddenly cold.

I start to write a couple of words for a poem,
scratch off one word, rumbling the sheet like a shirt
drenched in sweat and lamp smoke.
I stroke my uneven, day-old, unshaven jawbone.

Somewhere, Caitlin is calling. Somewhere,
beaches are calm. Somewhere, fishing boats
head towards home, nets wiggling with stories.
Somewhere, a man thinks he knows me;
he could not be further from the truth.

For, while people see me face the salt wind through a window,
no one knows the way to this home.

The Townspeople Thought I Knew the Weather

They all want to know if it is safe to hang the laundry,
or if the weather will hold for golf, or will the winds
be fair and wild as a new lover. But this is Swansea,
where it rains whenever it is not raining. As I was a lad
till now when I do not know any better, I am drenched
and leak whenever I enter a room, waterlogged,
smelling of soaked leaves.

They ask me what the weather is like, looking out
at the drenching rain. It is always better to lie
about such things and smile as a fox caught with a chicken
than to tell the god-awful truth—it is rain thick as carrots;
what else is new? Just give it a while or two.
The misery cannot keep up forever.
Every once in a while we catch a break.
If you live to be a hundred, you might see the skies open
and wonder what that blue stuff is.

I tell them to think of the small openings between showers;
the ones where we dodge quick as we can.
Those moments when familiarity
looks totally new again.

That never works, they tell me.
We take spoons of sunshine like it was bad medicine.
We hide when the day is swamped, dropping rain like tides.

Jumping into an Abyss

"Naked nerve and blood timid" —Dylan Thomas

When I settle within the silence of myself,
into the deepest region that is there,
a calm-like absence finds me
waiting, barefoot and lamb-calm, wetted down
by loss and restless-motionless.

It is then, and only then, I find myself
a stretching of nerve connecting nerve,
a weaving of messages,
electric voices and voids and sonic vibrations,
all blood gone wild, gone free, gone into particles
into the congress of everything
necessary and unnecessary.

And when I am like this,
I do not want to return to my original place
because this is where I belong—
a song worth singing
no one except me
wants to sing
aloud.

Dylan Thomas Walks from His Boyhood Home

He walked from the Uplands
through Singleton Park, then Brynmill Park
onto the bay, to Mumbles beach
where the windiest weather
tries to outdo itself with strong winds,
almost blowing itself out
with cheeks like Dizzy Gillespie
hitting a high note,
shattering the stratosphere
into pieces of chandelier glass diamonds.

All the greenness was overwhelming,
too much for any eye.
Here the loneliness was welcoming.
Silence was a new pair of shoes.
Wherever he walked, he kept things close
to his vest. Time was left behind
like sand dollars, crayfish in tidal pools,
or a fish, abandoned by a wave.

When he had too much of it,
when this quiet gnawed his tendons,
he went back the slow way
to the noise of the town.

He took what he brought,
which was nothing,
and left it behind.
When he came to his house,
he was not the same man
he had abandoned.
That man was long gone.

5 Cwmdonkin Drive, Swansea, Wales

Dylan Thomas's Birthplace

I could look out my bedroom window
to the edge of love.
The bay's curves are a tern in flight
to where I could not go.

I could dream through the day, and dreaming was free.
No boy should give up the comforts of his room
for the unknown,
unless it's a great adventure.

I would lie on my bed and look at the ceiling
like it was a blank sheet of paper
and compose the world around me,
editing carefully, choosing the right words
for the right occasions.
And there were many occasions to come.

I could not know it then, or sense it then
coming for me with opportunists
and tragedies, and the future I could not imagine.

But I was young and foolish like a polished apple.
I had a work of dreaming, and I plowed those fields.

Here my family moved upwards through society,
voices filling the rafters
with vowels. Mine was the timbre of a deep voice,
stilled within me, a secret storm.

I was young and easy then. Not more than a verse.
What could I know of dreaming,
having never exhausted mine? Darkness
was all around the house, coming up the walk,
ringing the doorbell—do not answer it, Mother,
it's me as an adult trying to find my way home.

Worm's Head

Where Dylan once got marooned by the tide
is probably not marked by a plaque or monument of any kind.
I will not visit there, for I am not the kind who ever does.
Where is Worm's Head? I will not know,
nor will I ever see it, for the sea brings only the stranded,
and I have no use for the sea.

Many times in this world, I have lost my place,
and many times I was put in my place, but neither suited me.
I am as strict as a sailboat through a narrow channel:
wheel turn and tack by the sail. I am the homebound kind,
far from my home, silent and cooperative in choppy seas.

Dylan Thomas's Chair,
Looking Out of the Writing Shed

White banners of egrets; lapwings'
slow irregular wingbeats, like a person
having a change of heart;
herons mating for life;
oystercatchers wading on the shore edges,
poking in the sand with long orange beaks;
seals suntanning on gray rocks,
merging with local color.

The oystercatchers knew this secret:
The world was a bipedal cockle.
If you pried it open
from its hinges
beyond its saltwater taste,
you might find sheen inside
like the inside of a pocket watch
with all the time in the world
to create.

Dylan Thomas's Writing Desk, Replica, at the Dylan Thomas Museum

1. Oil Lamp, Left Corner, Near the Window

The day smells of whale oil, smoky and turned down
like letters accumulating light. When the day ends,
make a new miniature sun, sprinkle its light
from a watering can, wavering with elbow movement.

And shall it be said, we could be our own God
controlling amount of radiance? Or shall it be said
we can be our own wet nurses, arms of towels,
running about, snipping sunlight into umbilical cords?
Or can it be said we could be our own roosters,
all fleshy red combs like sundown, raising our own ruckus,
trumpet and messenger and mailman with good news?
Or can it be said we can be our own parsons,
thumbing tides for catching our own fish, big as marlins?
We'd have enough to feed a nation of carried immigrants,
begging for a cross and communion and sparrows.

I am on fire, sheer tears of birds, trees of horizons,
an alto saxophone, panting with open jets of light.

2. Blue Notebook, Right of Oil Lamp

All I know is winter silence, shutters closing,
settling in, going on, no time
for opening a blue notebook.

I wander the ruins of darkness
mumbling poems, heartless and drifting
as snowflakes upwards into streetlights
with words for a God I can barely understand.

Hear the piano of softness, the parlors open
to strangest of strangers needing refuge,
yet no room for me, no room for sad me,
blue fingers rubbing the cold.

3. Pencils and Pens in a Glass Jar Near an Empty Brown Vase

The swans write across the water.
When the room cries for a blind man to wake up,
the light is a pen chasing dots of memory of where he is.
The wife coaxes the children into a corner
to stand tall as a narrow straight brown vase
picking the best of their pretty bright smiles
to place into flowers of movement.

There is a disruption in the clouds, opportunities fade.

4. Brown Empty Wine Bottle

I could drink your love—you sun; you flowers
with songs I hear in the night when everything
is so near and far away. I empty silence
and pour in the green force of beginnings
like a baby takes its first drop of milk, tentative
and tender, unsure what to expect next,
but trusting it will nourish—

lifting the lids off the chimneys
allowing all the dreams to gently speed away
to become stars just engaging the darkness
with voices.

5. Candies Near Full Ashtray and Small Cup

Sour lemon candy in wrappers
are waiting to poke out their suspicious heads.

Smudged and smacked, crumbled remains
of cigarettes reduced to stubs, smoked to filters,
some filters removed to get to the source directly.

A drinking cup is waiting for water
or wine or turtle eggs or echoes or rainwater.

What more do you need within easy reach?

The nearness of comfort,
a woman teasing the best of me
into the downy skin of absence.

6. Scattered Worksheet, Notes, Gull Feather, Dictionary

Spread as peacock feathers, or a deck of cards
by a card shark, or rays out of the cornerstone of the sun,
or moon through empty branches, or bristles
of a broomstick used so much the spread
is uneven and worn as a pair of old shoes.

The necessary is exposed like an open blouse.

The vocabulary of forgotten words drizzle,
as a shepherd in the fall of his season
bringing the flock to the candlelight
to shear what had gathered into fullness.

7. Looking Outside the Window

Looking outside the window
into the story of the sea,
where did we go, you and me?

If I walked outside the turning of the leaves,
and if I stepped across the sea,
would your arms
still find me?

And if the sea should go empty
as a begging bowl,
would you still feed me
with apples
peeled in a red bowl
that I could offer one
to the man starving
on the street
just below.

I could lie
in your arms all night,
and the world would not care.
The cherry blossoms
would simply fill the air.

I am light
in your arms.
You can't feel me.
You carry me inside you,
as a secret yellow stone.

I walk and part darkness,
removing rose thorns.
I sneak past windows
subtle as a storm.

You hardly notice me.
I am the one who sings
as the night,
searching for answers
in the absence of light.

I can never
in all this lonely world
strike a match
this bitter cold.

Inseparable

"Through my small, bonebound island I have learnt all I know,
experienced all, and sensed all.
All I write is inseparable from the island."
—Dylan Thomas

Why separate what is connected? We cannot.
The teeth of life and life work are twined by fine thread.

An island is a skeleton in a sea of constellations, floating.
What holds it together is firm as a wisp of wind.

When I was young enough not to know better, I thought I knew it all.
Now, I am as old as the smallest, and I know less.

After I was born, my life hardened into rock,
worn down by the sea.

Each grain of sand is a part of me. Each transcribes deeply
into me and is still being written, silently.

All the days pass as stars, tiny as minnows following silence.
I find myself a part of them, parting from them, into the sea.

Getting It Right

"To write anything, just to let the words and ideas,
the half-forgotten images, tumble on the sheets of paper"
—Dylan Thomas

A villanelle

Do not lose your way for the lack of words.
We are ships losing our way.
We are fragile as paper and hearts stirred.

Loneliness is a thirsty bird.
We need to see what will happen, what life will say.
Do not lose your way for the lack of words.

Your ideas are tumbling like loose boards.
We are stillness across a long bay,
we are fragile as paper and hearts stirred.

Day breaks many backs, greening the dark yards.
Take this hand, these words of blue jays.
Do not lose your way for the lack of words.

We do not need to measure our words in thirds,
where each step is dangerous prey.
We are fragile as paper and hearts stirred.

And what is it, exactly, we think we heard?
Do not lose one moment, one day,
do not lose your way for the lack of words.
We are fragile as paper and hearts stirred.

After the First Death

"After the first death, there is no other" —Dylan Thomas,
A Refusal to Mourn the Death, By Fire, of a Child in London

1.

Death comes, we think, not for us,
but for someone else, and we are surprised
to find, to our chagrin, it was for us—

not sound, not soundless, but somewhere
between, pain and the emptying,
poured out, either tablespoon or

flash flood, or between, never one
or the other, but other-less, then
we know no moment afterwards,

words can hardly speak, speechless
we enter what cannot be exited,
and what we feel cannot be known.

2.

Is this it? Our hearts are so callous,
we lose track of all the many more
dying. Is there some room for pity
for corpses? We turn our heads away
like a stray weathervane
not knowing which way the wind blows,
twisting like a dagger in a stone heart,
refusing to mourn again and again.

After the second, do we count
with numb fingers, wrenching hearts
out of the clouds, yanking stars,
hands holding fire, not feeling flame,

not remembering the first name
or the third. And more fall,

none rise, no one cries
like an ambulance, death riding
in the back checking pulses.
We forget and we remember
and we try to forget and we try
to remember, our feet slosh
through floods of blood,
and we do not notice
if it is ours or someone else's
or if it matters anymore
or if anyone even cares
we are no longer there.

We do not notice this;
no one does. There is no accountant
adding grief on a ledger,
no one held accountable,
numbers just numb us, make us less
than what we were,
numbers do not have flame anymore
and we are spoken of
as if we were dead in our tracks,

and maybe we are. Maybe,
we never mattered, never counted.
Maybe, the one with the most skulls
loses, the ones with less pain, win,
or some rule like that,

I am never sure
because I am still stuck
looking at the first body
like it is me
while others wonder
does it matter?

Someone said, we all count
or none of us count. Someone says,
some count more than others;
you can count on it.

Hundreds, no, thousands, no, more—
no one seems to care and it never ends.
There is a greed for more.
There never seems to be a way out.

Only one way out, says another, die.
So more die, pyramids of skulls,
all speaking about what it is like
to be flame, to be loss, forgotten.

No one hears them; we're too busy dying.
We all have to die someday,
someone says, firing into shadows.
It is easy to kill shadows,

it is harder to be killed by shadows,
to not know why you had to die
this moment, this day, this way,
bullets punctuating a serious end.

This child I hold, all burnt
like a last fall leaf, cannot tell us
what it is like to be first and not last,
as they headed to a class they'd never attend.

I tend to the absence
although he is gone to ash,
his bones still singing
pain while others fall like steady rain.

4.

Is this it? Is this all there is?
Someone please tell me that this is not true.
Someone please lie to me
that peace is just around the corner,
that all we need is a good negotiator
and a willingness to stop—

but madness is contagious.
One conflict looks like it is simmering
to a collapse, another springs up
as wildfire, whole populations
of fiery speeches, all flammable tongues,
all dropping accusations
like bombs, like they cared less
about rational behavior, once kindled
they just add kerosene.

This is not a child I hold
but a bomb that did not explode
and the only thing preventing it
from going off
is the fact I am holding it together
like a promise.

Some say, there is no child;
it is a metaphor. Then why is it crying:
lips flaking, tears of ash,
dying its green last days?

This is the problem with prophecy.
No one can see
what they do not want to see.
And if you complain and warn,
they call you insane.
And if the child is a bonfire,

then they simply deny
they had any reason
to sharpen their teeth
and call for action
when sometimes, inaction is called for.

Already, people are marching to drums
where there are no drums,
just the blaze of drums,
just the flares in their eyes,
all caution thrown into conflagration winds.

5.

"There is no death after the first death,"
should be in the news. Troops withdraw
behind imaginary lines someone once drew

and no one remembers who.
There are no statues erected in honor
of anyone who needlessly had to die.

Someone starts burying weapons
instead of bodies. Children start playing
peacemaker. Of course, some will object.

The ones with war contracts will lose business.
The ones who salivate over war maps
will have to curb their insatiable appetites.

What would everyone do if peace broke out
and everyone got it. There would be no cure
for happiness and a good night's sleep.

What if, there was no first death?
What if the craziness ended in a straightjacket?
A person can dream, can't they?

6.

Did you ever look steadily into flame?
Into the eye-storm, the essence of blue?
You can smell sulfur and cherry blossoms
and moondust and beginning of life.
Look into the needle-eye of flame
until it is hypnotic and seducing.
Do you, do you dare? There is no
turning back once you enter the gateway
to another world, where it is beyond
what you expect. It looks like a child's eye.
The child can see the flame coming.
There is no stopping it.
It is already in their eyes, like an explosion.
A flash—then no more no more.

7.

There are skulls falling out of the sky
like bombs, like campaign slogans,
like promises no one keeps.

However, the one promise they keep
is that after the first death
there will be more.

Restless, restless, beats the cold heart
in the one calling the shots
and never has to pull the trigger.

Now the bombs look like flaming children
falling like autumn red leaves,
like trace bullets, like death songs.

8.

When my child was born, it was like
a comet fell out of the sky.
How fragile he looked.

I touched his skull to make sure he was real.
His skull was still forming, after being squeezed.
The bonding began old as ancient times.

I made promises to keep him from being harmed.
How little I understood the world.
How impossibly big and changeable it seemed.

Like one birth, one promise, could make a difference.
I had to try, didn't I?

Time Takes Me out of the Shadow of My Hand

Waking by the childhood fireplace,
I notice the newspaper on my lap
nestling as a cat digging claws to find its place
of comfort. My wife is knitting quietness
in a chair, rocking herself with a pleasant breath.
Nearby the children are quietly playing
with their shadows like paper doll cutouts.

I am growing older as the days come shorter,
and the days are restlessly greening
in the shadow of first snow.
Each moment is going slower as I count time,
trying to remember what I can
before it all disappears
up the stairs to sleepy beds.

Each morning when I wake up,
I should thank each new day.
If I fall down on my promises,
keep me tilted the right way.
For I am aging; and the boy I was
is running further from me,
casting long shadows,
filling the wind with his songs
like a lantern lighting the way.

This Is Not a Classical Bach Movement; This Is Persecution, Again and Again

For the Swansea Bay Asylum Seekers Support Group and
its sister charities, and thinking of our own inner conflicts
from pro-immigrant and anti-immigrant groups in America.
Section titles are based on sections in the anthology of women
asylum seekers, *Fragments From The Dark*, edited by
Jeni Williams and Latéfa Guémar.

1. Homelessness

We come from unsettling shores
in boats stuffed to the walls—
no room to move, no baggage at all.

All we could carry was ourselves,
the rest we left behind,
trying to forget.

We left bombed villages,
the destroyed roads,
the dying, the desperate, the disease.

We left some of our family,
friends, and our enemies.
We left what we knew for a place we knew not.

The sea tossed our stomachs,
the crew took our money,
we took great risks going nowhere—

to be hated, to be chased, to be protested,
to go hungry, to have no shelter,
no place to rest that was not shattered.

They said this place would be better;
they were wrong, or lying.
We all heard of this great place,

but we are not allowed to settle.
We are hated again. The world is vicious;
not one religion lets us stay and helps us.

When we were in a war-torn land, at least
we knew the enemy who moved among us,
and persecuted us. Here, we did not expect it.

2. Afraid to Look Back, Afraid to Look Forward

Did the secret police follow us? Did our friends
tell them where to find us in exchange for favors
or to avoid arrest? Sleep is restlessly borderless.

Did the trees grow eyes? Did someone pull fingernails?
Does the opposition have rational? Does anyone?
Or is the world looking backward, to a sterner way?

Or is the world afraid to look forward toward a better way?
People have been killing each other for generations,
for reasons large and small, and sometimes for no reason at all.

Today, my shadow follows me, keeping notes on my activities.
Tomorrow is crossing the border, keeping on the run.
We do not know where to look, nothing is really safe.

We close our eyes, hope for the best, bullets raining overhead.
Where we are going, we never know. We are always on the go.
We are not allowed to stay here, or there, or anywhere.

I wear the same clothes; I eat sadness like cakes;
I sleep running through minefields; I find my way
to no place where I can find my own, dreaming like a stone.

3. *Arriving and Not Arriving*

I know when I am not wanted; it is written on your faces.
The memories I miss are simple: a rose; a house of stone;
a kettle making soup out of potatoes and chicken bones.

There was a gate; I could close every day,
until they destroyed it and the dog limped away.
The people I could count on were killed trying to escape.

When I left, I left a part of me, waiting on a stoop.
All that was left of my house, reduced to kindling.
I ran from the reddening fields and non-stop killing.

When I reached here, scared and alone,
the first person I met cursed me, casting stones,
hitting my face until it sagged and swooped.

When does someone arrive?
Where do they find a safe place?
When will they realize I almost died?

Epistle to the Displaced

Peace to you in a place where there is no peace,
where grace has no meaning, and you hide
from the violence where there is no shelter.
Where you are is so dangerous, so uncertain,
there is no guarantee this message will reach you
or ease your fears. And I fear, you have died
or lay dying under ruins, wondering
where salvation is, where peace is promised,
and have you the grace necessary to go there.

Where I am, is safe for the moment, but
as we both know, not one moment is certain
or safe, and all my security could be gone,
wiped out in an instant, and my light taken.
So as grace leaves me in search of you,
you shall be making a different peace,
one before death, wiping the slate clean,
professing your faults, as the pieces of life
disassemble around you, lacking grace.

Copperopolis

The unofficial name of Swansea, Wales, because
of its copper mines

The day is being excavated
where no one walks the sand
to the dark caves of our hearts,
to strike rocks into catalysts of night-stars.

When he is done mining,
the morning does not wake, it coughs.
He heads to where no one sleeps,
no one wanders alone in the corridors.

Here the local copper is endless as pennies.
These excesses have made this town what it is today—
a place where no one wants to be
with copper smelts burning the night.

*

They can try to fancy up Swansea,
but still this is dank-town at its worst—
common as laverbread, or cockles from the bay,
or salt-marsh lamb raised in the estuary.

What does he know of culture?
He knows the high-heat
of a cauldron wearing down metal
into thin copper.

He knows a place hotter than a million suns
or the anger of a man
taking more than he can,
where copper looks and smells like blood.

Copper is soft and malleable
as flesh turned into electrical conductivity.
He cannot interpret these messages,
having lost his faith during the great revival.

Copper has a reddish-orange color
and the same tolerance to heat as people do.
Sometimes, the copper turns aquamarine
because it is the byproduct of earth, sky, and stars.

Copper work is making him old before his time,
as blackened and agitated as a shadow moving.
This is hellish work. Someone has to do it
so the rich can settle into their villas.

They build there, away from this stench.
They do not have to see him
churning as a cauldron,
working hard as a heart.

*

He can see the limestone cliffs from his house,
the sand dunes and salt marches
with wading birds
looking for oysters on the Loughor Estuary.

His wife is making laverbread out of seaweed,
the only thing they can afford.
He opens one of the cockles
and finds copper instead of a pearl.

Falling in Love, Becoming a Desperate Man

It was painful, wanting
for what I could not have, staring tongue-
tied-numb in the lack of wellness.

I could not have what was far away.
I was too afraid to ask, my face skewed
as a person out of touch with his pain.

As she passed as close as a moon,
I could not taste the sound
of cherry blossoms opening as her smile.

All I could see was blurry, in a rush,
speaking strange languages in my heart,
and I could not repeat a phrase.

As she kept going, I kept thinking,
what it would be like to be with her,
how it would never be.

This Is Perfectly Clear

The sea has fallen upon bad times,
kicked from home to home.

The raven ominously sings black notes
the forthcoming fury.

The way out is painfully clear:
We are out of tune.

When we come together, we clash—
like rose-light makes music.

Glass is stained by lack of harmony.
When the body is fire-bombed,

heart reduced by acetylene torches,
and not one shattered hope remains,

the heart is a cardinal
bringing crayons of song.

On This Day, Many Will Die

"Death Has No Dominion" —Dylan Thomas

1.

The storms do not care they unload
nasty secrets. Like it was all it could do:
releasing dark-blood of a wounded animal,
spools of loss. This storm thrashed starlings out.
Air moved rivers of birds, ebbing,
closing together, like through a narrowing.
Congealing as the storm continued to die.
The sky has a shotgun hole of blue, struggling,
a fading heart refusing its last moments.
It seeks the most sincere form of death poses.

2.

I went to see you at your deathbed. I lied,
suggesting you looked better.
You were skeleton words.
Rasps of antlers on winter trees made more noise.
You looked awful. Like a mountain fell
shrieking on top of you. What held you together?
Mere spite, or it was not your time yet?
I tend to consider the first option. Too mean
to die; too stubborn to give up your anger.
Whatever kindness you were born with
simply became empty as picked apple branches
when you were born. You set the land-speed record.
A short fuse, cocked as a lightning bolt.
Even Death was afraid of your wicked ways.

3.

All day, the deer shed its responsibilities
as life spilled out as sunsets. Its eye not closing,
not wanting to stop seeing the world.
It decided this life's harshness
when peeled down like bark off a tree,
was not so bad after all. It was late to learn this.
It leaned into shadows. The rain was full
of ducks calling in the passing storm.

The deer could forgive the hunters,
finally reaching him,
if he knew how, actually had words for forgiveness.
If he could speak while breath struggled
like a person grabbing sheets fighting death,
he'd say: *If all battles were easy,*
the struggle would not be so hard.

4.

In dying light, distant thunder
like cardio paddles jumpstarting hearts.
In the forest of death, breath leaps
as a shot nine-point deer, and falls,
dragging, limping, leaving blood spoors.
In a hospital a person grinds his teeth
resisting with all they have left.
Death does no kindness for these.

5.

When starlings reassembled
in the tree's antlers, the sky quieting
with no pulse, the postmortem
should have read: *You died, heartless.*

There was no truth in that statement.
They could actually see it swollen
and clogged. Fatty foods will do that.

You asked me to hunt deer for you.
You know I hate guns.

Your anger rained.
I think that is what took you out.
Certainly, death did not want you.
Probably when you tried to go to heaven,
you were barred; and when you went to hell,
you were not welcome there.

In the next life,
I hope you become a stag or storm cloud
or starling or tree or learn kindness.

Knowing our luck, you'd come back even worse.

Where Is the Sun This Morning?

I would ask the ferryboat,
but it was swallowed by the sea.
The brick buildings do not tell where the sun went;
they closed their eyes with lowered shades.

A miner coughing up dust
is straddling a blaze-white sky.
He carries a pickaxe, lifting it with tattooed arms.
He claims he the saw the sun in the tunnel,
near the rails for the coal,
going one way, all the way to China.
But he is as drunk as a groom getting confidence
to spend his first night with his wife,
spinning in circles, world slanting, pockets
of notes on what to say when alone,
wondering if his words are kind enough,
will she judge them, or will she leave him.

Where is the sun? It is late in the day.

The girl finding pansies for her hair
twists them in a garland; she
cannot see what she is doing.
Her fingers work from memory.
She seems to have the knack.
She sits on a wicker chair
with holes like Swiss cheese,
saying she misses the light
through the chair's knotted openings
like fledglings waiting to be fed.

The sun is not where it belongs.

Letter to Caitlin, a Love Poem

Dylan Thomas met Caitlin Macnamara in 1936

1.

Do you remember the night we met
in the Wheatsheaf pub in London?
They say, when I laid my head on your lap I was drunk—
but I was really drunk with love.

You were a dancer that danced into my heart,
and there you shall dance forever.

No matter how many women they say
I would stray to like a lost dog,
I would return to you like an annual,
like a north star for a sailor,
like a lamp with blinding blue flame.

They say, I drunkenly proposed that night,
but I was staring into the swirl in your eyes.
I was swallowed into them, like a forthcoming,
like a sea swell in the orchestra of night,
and though I clung to the ropes of reality,
I let go into your face of pure light.

2.

Do you remember when we married in Penzance?
How we tore into each other like piñatas,
spilling our love on the counters, the bear rug,
the crystal chandelier casting diamond light in your hair?

We were stormy, drenching with star juice, moon halves,
almonds, and castaway fragments of belief.

And it was worth it, wasn't it, to burn like that?

3.

When I die, bury me in the churchyard in Laugharne.
Carry my casket like it was a bouquet of lilies.
Return my body to the earth where I shall kiss it.
Remember me when you look out at the sea.

The Force That Stirs Stillness

**Based on the Dylan Thomas poem, "The Force that
Through the Green Fuse Drives the Flower"**

The force that stirs stillness
in water
is not a voice
nor silence opening
flowers in morning
disappearing
as light

absence pushes awe
aside
like a birth
into the forever

Below the Beech, above the Tâf

Painting by Guy Manning

I would lie on my back, looking into leaves
until the world was out of focus,
pointless dots for impressionistic painters.

What I was doing was seeing beyond
what we were meant to see and *seeing*.

As the trees became blurred lines
I could see right through them.
The world beyond was no longer invisible
or strange, or faraway, or impossible to get to.

The real world, the one we are not meant to see,
has been hidden and hard to imagine.

I return there, whenever I can.
Age never stopped me; I always Believe.
A part of me is already in that ghostly Other World.

Dylan Thomas in the Dark

Under the ash tree, he smokes
down to ash
letting stars out of his chest.

He is not from the neighborhood of known.
It is as if he was not ever there
among the row houses or the breeze.

I thought I saw him,
his hair curly with ash leaves,
but it must have been my imagination.

Among silence and lack of wind,
the man I saw was never there,
but I feel his whistling in my bones.

Dylan Thomas by the Bay

Based on a photograph taken at the Boat House, Laugharne,
July 1953, months before he died

The estuary of the River Tâf
is as quiet as an egg. The water
against the rowboats is not heard.
The sand sifting is silent. Not
one wing in the air disturbs.

The pen makes no sound
scribbling on the surface
of a paper, leaving a tattoo
of absence and gone things
forgotten, set aside, away.

Wait patiently for inspiration to happen.
Leaves and wildflowers hold their breath.

Coda: Dylan Thomas and the Newspaper Article Found Inside His Wallet When He Died

For Jeni, my guide to Dylan and Swansea

When Dylan died,
he had one newspaper article about himself
folded in his wallet
like a black-lipped pearl oyster hides a black pearl.

It must have been special to him;
he carried it like a talisman
to every poetry reading, every hotel, every beach,
every corner meeting—
everywhere—his whole life.

It was a picture of him winning a footrace in school.
He would point at it and say,
Look, I was not always chubby.

But with Dylan, there were truths
and truths within truths
and he loved telling a great lie.

The truth is
it was a handicapped race.

No, he was not handicapped. It means something different.

He was expected to run a mile track
and he had a three-quarter head start.

All through his life he would find shortcuts—
don't we all?

Here was Dylan proud of his one accomplishment
that had zilch to do with poetry:
it was about accomplishment.

Stained Glass Finalists

III

Stained Glass Based on Dylan Thomas's Poems, Stories, Plays

The University of Wales Trinity Saint David in Swansea, Wales, had two international contests. One was for poetry and the other was for stained glass. The university has a degree in both programs.

There were 65 entries, with 21 stained glass finalists on display. Each one of the stained glass pieces had to be based on a Dylan Thomas poem, story, or quote, and related to the theme of "Harmony." The titles for the poems are the titles of the pieces of stained glass art.

Harmony on Fern Hill

Stained glass by J. H. Blaylock

The contour map of Fern Hill is seasonal
and topical heights and valleys—
you can almost rub your fingers
on its flat surface and feel the rise
and fall of earth's chest, relaxing.
This world is a coherence of opposites
meeting and repelling.

We need to find commonality
to negotiate our differences
passing through generations
like a bad inheritance.
Someone needs to realize the insanity of arguing
and expecting different outcomes. Surely, people
remember the calm days of their childhood
when problems never troubled their world
and the sky stared back with mercy. Now,
children know no peace,
the sky falls on their heads.

Someone needs to talk about the madness.
Someone needs to point to another way,
like it was a map to reasonable thinking,
and say, there it is.

High Street under the Moon

Stained glass by S.I. Gray

There is a dark mood. Tempers flare,
torching the moon into bloodstone.
The ebb always retreats.
Anger passes in quarter phases.
What seemed a dead-end street
where streetlights failed to reach
has a small niche of light.
When you think the worst is coming, actually
another day is coming.

Tonight, tidal waves smooth on your face.

"I Have Longed to Move Away from This Ugly, Lovely Town"

Stained glass by M. Mativi
Also a quote by Dylan Thomas about his birthplace,
Swansea, Wales

Birds recall sad music
on a perfect morning
when the town puts on its makeup
or races to tidy its tie
into a perfect knot

we put on appearances
for appearance sake
making ourselves better
than we are

every time I try to leave
slamming the door
like it was a last breath
I find myself back in the same room
grooming myself
in the mirror
not seeing myself
as I am

I cannot leave
no matter how much I cannot stand
this misery
it loves my company

I know better

the leaving stays

Ribbed between Desert and Water Storm

Stained glass by M. Fagan

When we meet, we merge into ribbed light
holding the lungs of forgiveness.
When we meet, we ripple and follow
each other and blend together
with alchemical kisses, making lines
across a desert where the wind is sifting sand
into a snaking smile, always fleeting.
Like waves on a shore moving coastlines,
retreating, leaving, and abandoning,
what we do not need
is more pain or sorrow.

When storms move their fingers across the sky,
messaging the rains into letting go,
what remains afterwards is stillness:
rain soft as a person sorry they hurt someone.
When the person expresses regret
and they mean it, love ripples—
repeating the apology.
Like geese following the lead,
we should all work together
to get to where we need to go.

Echoes of Fern Hill

Stained glass by L. Marouf

I am thrilled by light. It reverberates
like a glass of water,
a long, lingering ting.

The hills are like this—shimmering shook
ricocheting sound
rigorous as a swim in ice water.

Sound amasses with memories,
heaping upon each recollection,
a concert finding the pinnacle.

And when the audience of trees and hills
folds its program notes,
the silence becomes a different composition.

Harmony of Childhood Dreams—Fern Hill

Stained glass by M. LeBreton

I am almost awake and almost asleep, drift
less as a boat without rudder or sail or harbor
to set anchor or slip away from.

I am under a blanket of owl wings.
In the forest of dark beliefs, I use
the current to swoop on
to the unsuspecting
like light arriving earlier than normal.

I am the horses peering around the edge
of sleep like it was a hill with ferns
numerous as thoughts
keeping the morning and night
from meeting and unsettling.

I am colors finding their way home
after being in the lost.

Though Lovers Be Lost, Love Shall Not

Stained glass by S. Healy

A Shakespearian sonnet

We may lose our way from time to time, but not our love.
We may seek what we cannot find, but love finds us.
If we think love has forgotten or abandoned us, shoved
us to the side, it has not. Love is where the winds rush
to find the edge of the earth and find a willing heart.
We shall not forget when we find love or lose love,
nor shall we forget when we find ourselves apart
from love. As new lovers cannot get enough hugs
and seeing clouds in each other's eyes, it never is enough.
We shall lose each other many times, many times be found.
Keeping love alive seems hard, and it can be rough
to keep the romance. But love is never a line, it is round
cycling moons and suns, rising and falling and kissing.
It never goes away, it is never dormant, it is never failing.

Balance

Stained glass by R. Griskonyte

Chaos and symmetry

opposite poles finding their way amid a neutral field
where we come together

we need to break
patterns into pieces for a stained glass
of convergence, light through
the cathedral of the heart
where the astonished
genuflect

we study too much the lack of balance
creating a negative energy and adding to it

as it accumulates
exponentially
anger feeds off fear
ravenous
insatiable

the best way to find the equilibrium
is to hold peace in your heart
like it was an olive branch
carried from the most distant safe shore
we begin to row to

Flow

Stained glass by C. Brown

We want to drift in and out of peace
just awakening, the theme of silence in our lives.
Streams of light like floating robes of herons.

We must search for peace like we had a douser
to find harmony in ourselves.
The most basic of all desires is being comforted.

Like winds find their way towards merging
into a single breath, one that moves
without moving with the sacred stream,

where is balance in our lives?
When light and dark meet, and merge
into twilight and dusk, neither gives in.

Eventually one overwhelms.
All relationships need surrender into trust.
When we flow, there are no boundaries.

Tree of Life

Stained glass by M. Davies

When we were still trees translating into people,
the world was less complicated. We could cross-pollinate:
making a connection, simple as an apple
making stars inside the core of love.

It was simple then to keep assurances.
Temptation was not in our vocabulary. Our branches
reached towards the heavens as wild hair.
The jar of the sky opened its mouth, sighing.

Now, the world is troubled. We forgot how to share.
We are no longer rooted in the blessedness of soil and love.
We shed tears as bark. Birds fly out of the domed sky
into the stars, warning the heavens of our loss.

It is never too late. The leaves are still returning.
Branches wave, come on back.
Love is always serious about digging into the surface.
Patience is needed when revival of love is forthcoming.

Cwmdonkin Park across from Dylan Thomas's House

Final Note:

Dylan Thomas is perhaps the first multimedia writer. He wrote newspaper articles, made live radio broadcasts, appeared on stage, and wrote plays, fiction, and, of course, poetry. He was 39 years old when he died in New York City after a poetry reading and allegedly drinking too much. But the myth of Dylan was in place that night, and the truth of his death is he died an entirely different way.

Dylan Thomas wrote 100 poems and 30 short stories, as well as radio and film scripts and plays, with such important material as *Under Milk Wood*, "Do Not Go Gentle into the Night," "Fern Hill," "And Death Shall Have No Dominion," "The Force That Through the Green Fuse Drives the Flower," "Poem in October," "A Child's Christmas In Wales," and others.

He was the original bohemian poet living the original "fast and furious" lifestyle, the man who would "live fast and die young." He influenced Bob Zimmerman to change his name to Bob Dylan and the Beatles to appear on their classic "Sgt. Pepper" album cover peeking over Tom Mix's Stetson. He also influenced the Beat poets like Allen Ginsberg.

Dylan lived through two world wars and the threat of nuclear war. He saw the bombing of his hometown of Swansea. He was not the myth he helped to create, for a person is always more than one thing. Dylan Thomas was many things, and all of them were eclectic, full of images, raging "against the dying of the light."

I wish to thank the University of Wales Trinity Saint David; its Vice Chancellor, Professor Medwin Hughes, DL; Dr. Jeni Williams, Senior Lecturer, Literature and Creative Writing Academic Director, MA Creative Writing; Dr. Menna Elfyn, writer and bard; Dr. Grahame Davies, poet and novelist; Hanna Ellis, Dylan's granddaughter; Eleri Benyon, Head of Corporate Communications and PR, who told me "Cwmdonkin—the w is sounded like oo and the rest quite phonetic—*Coom-don-kin*. You'll get to meet lots of Welsh speakers who'll be happy to help!"; Mr. Paul Osborne, who took me to the Swansea Quaker Meeting on Sunday morning and for lunch at the Dragon Brasserie; Jeff Towns, author, owner of the Dylan Thomas Bookstore in Swansea, publisher of Dylan Thomas, and chairman of the Dylan Thomas Society of Great Britain; Dr. Kristie Bohanta, who provided a ride to my program and her clutch went; Geoff Haden, who provided a special tour of the Dylan Thomas birthplace; the wait staff during the award ceremony at the Waterfront Museum, who asked me to read my poem to them—and how could I refuse as Dylan would have liked me to do that; and the various people I met along the way who told me Dylan Thomas stories and made me feel welcome.

The two paintings by Guy Manning appeared in the same tenth issue of *The Lampeter Review* as my two poems appeared.

Acknowledgments

About Place Journal: "This Is Not a Classical Bach Movement; This Is Persecution, Again and Again (part #1 and #3")

Black Poppy Review: "Dylan Thomas in the Dark"

Blue Heron Review: "The Force That Stirs Stillness"

Cahaba River Literary Journal: "Tree of Life"

Festival Writer: "Worm's Head," "Where Is the Sun This Morning?"

Flutter House: "Dylan Thomas by the Bay," "Jumping Into an Abyss"

The Furious Gazelle: "Ribbed between Desert and Water Storm," "Balance"

Kentucky Review: "Above the Spring Tâf," "Coda," "Dylan Thomas at the Writing Shed," "Dylan Thomas Chair, Looking Out the Writing Shed," "Harmony on Fern Hill," "Letter to Caitlin, a Love Poem," "The Townspeople Thought I Knew the Weather"

New Verse News: "Epistle to the Displaced"

Poppy Road Review: "Below the Beech, Above the Tâf," "Inseparable," "Secrets"

Turtle Island Quarterly: "After the First Death"

Watershed: "The Boat House and the Dylan Thomas Writing Shed"

The Whirlwind Review: "Flow," "Harmony of Childhood Dreams—Fern Hill"

Writer's Monthly: "Dylan Thomas's Writing Shed at the Boat House," "Dylan Thomas in the Writing Shed in Candle Light"

"This Is Perfectly Clear" appeared in *Switch (the Difference)* (Kind of a Hurricane Press, 2014).

The author received the 2014 Dylan Thomas International Poetry Award for his poem "Daffodils" (The University of Wales Trinity Saint David).

Cover artwork, "Dylan Thomas Writing Shed" by Matthew Watkeys; author photo by Linda Griggs; cover and interior book design by Diane Kistner; Adobe Jensen Pro text and titling

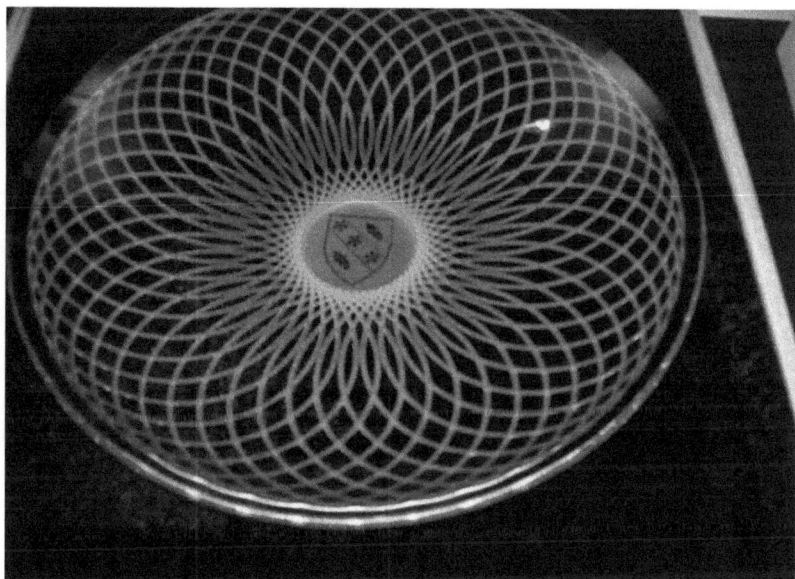

2014 Dylan Thomas International Poetry Award, Glass Bowl

About FutureCycle Press

FutureCycle Press is dedicated to publishing lasting English-language poetry books, chapbooks, and anthologies in both print-on-demand and Kindle ebook formats. Founded in 2007 by long-time independent editor/publishers and partners Diane Kistner and Robert S. King, the press incorporated as a nonprofit in 2012. A number of our editors are distinguished poets and writers in their own right, and we have been actively involved in the small press movement going back to the early seventies.

The FutureCycle Poetry Book Prize and honorarium is awarded annually for the best full-length volume of poetry we publish in a calendar year. Introduced in 2013, our Good Works projects are anthologies devoted to issues of universal significance, with all proceeds donated to a related worthy cause. Our Selected Poems series highlights contemporary poets with a substantial body of work to their credit; with this series we strive to resurrect work that has had limited distribution and is now out of print.

We are dedicated to giving all of the authors we publish the care their work deserves, making our catalog of titles the most diverse and distinguished it can be, and paying forward any earnings to fund more great books.

We've learned a few things about independent publishing over the years. We've also evolved a unique, resilient publishing model that allows us to focus mainly on vetting and preserving for posterity poetry collections of exceptional quality without becoming overwhelmed with bookkeeping and mailing, fundraising activities, or taxing editorial and production "bubbles." To find out more about what we are doing, come see us at www.futurecycle.org.

The FutureCycle Poetry Book Prize

All full-length volumes of poetry published by FutureCycle Press in a given calendar year are considered for the annual FutureCycle Poetry Book Prize. This allows us to consider each submission on its own merits, outside of the context of a contest. Too, the judges see the finished book, which will have benefitted from the beautiful book design and strong editorial gloss we are famous for.

The book ranked the best in judging is announced as the prize-winner in the subsequent year. There is no fixed monetary award; instead, the winning poet receives an honorarium of 20% of the total net royalties from all poetry books and chapbooks the press sold online in the year the winning book was published. The winner is also accorded the honor of being on the panel of judges for the next year's competition; all judges receive copies of all contending books to keep for their personal library.